LOVE LOVES FEAR

"I know you're tired but come, this is the way...

In your light I learn how to love.

In your beauty, how to make poems.

You dance inside my chest where no-one sees you,

but sometimes I do, and that sight becomes this art."

JALALUDDIN RUMI

LOVE LOVES FEAR

Barb Ryan

Illustrations by Alysse Hennessey

Printed in the USA
ISBN: 978-1-943190-11-9

Ordering Information:
If you are interested in quantity sales for your organization, please contact Barb Ryan at barbr@efn.org.

Wild Ginger Press
www.wildgingerpress.com

I dedicate this book to the Divine Loving Light that surrounds us all and is within each of us. May we feel and know the presence of Love.

LOVE

LOVE
LOVES
EVERYTHING.

LOVE SURROUNDS EVERYTHING.

LOVE IS WITHIN EVERYTHING.

LOVE IS ALL THERE IS.

LOVE LOVES EVERYTHING, INCLUDING FEAR.

FEAR

FEAR FEARS EVERYTHING, ESPECIALLY LOVE.

WHEN LOVE APPROACHES FEAR, FEAR GETS REALLY BIG AND ANGRY...

TRYING TO SCARE LOVE AWAY.

LOVE IS PATIENT.

LOVE IS KIND.

LOVE LOVES.

LOVE LOVES FEAR.
LOVE BEAMS LOVE AT FEAR.

FEAR IS SO SCARED

~~~~~~~~~~~

THAT IT RUNS AWAY.

RUNS AND RUNS ...
AS FAST AS IT CAN
TO ALL CORNERS OF
THE EARTH.

NO MATTER WHERE IT RUNS

LOVE IS THERE.

LOVE IS PATIENT.

LOVE IS KIND.

LOVE LOVES FEAR.

LOVE BEAMS
LOVE AT FEAR.

THIS SCARES FEAR
SO MUCH
THAT IT SHRINKS
INTO A TINY DOT.

LOVE
LOVE IS PATIENT.
LOVE IS KIND.
LOVE LOVES FEAR.
LOVE BEAMS LOVE AT FEAR.

FEAR SURROUNDED
BY LOVE SURRENDERS
~~~~~~~~~~
TO ITS WARM EMBRACE.

FEAR IS TRANSFORMED AND BECOMES

~~~~~~~~~~~~

PART OF LOVE.